GREEK & ROMAN MYTHOLOGY

GREEK & ROMAN MYTHOLOGY

DOVERPICTURA

DOVER PUBLICATIONS, INC. | Mineola, New York

By Alan Weller.
Designed by Joel Waldrep.

Greek & Roman Mythology is a new work, first published by Dover Publications, Inc., in 2008.

The CD-ROM file names correspond to the images in the book. All of the artwork stored on the CD-ROM can be imported directly into a wide range of design and word-processing programs on either Windows or Macintosh platforms. No further installation is necessary.

ISBN 10: 0-486-99028-1
ISBN 13: 978-0-486-99028-6
Manufactured in the United States of America
Dover Publications, Inc., 31 East 2nd Street, Mineola, NY 11501
www.doverpublications.com

009

010

013

014 background

019

020

021

027

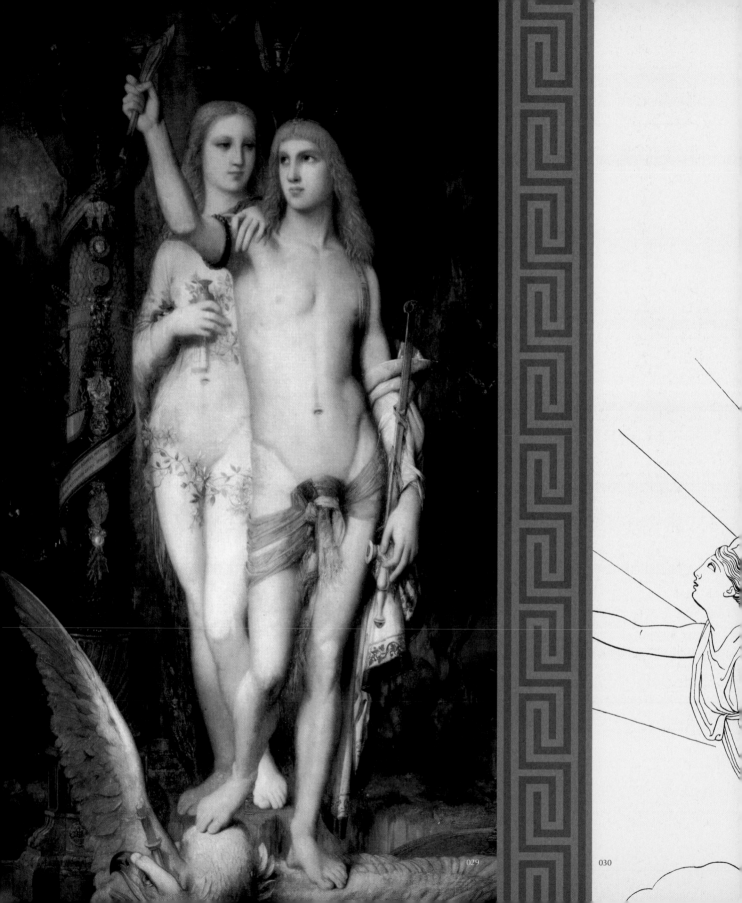

031

032

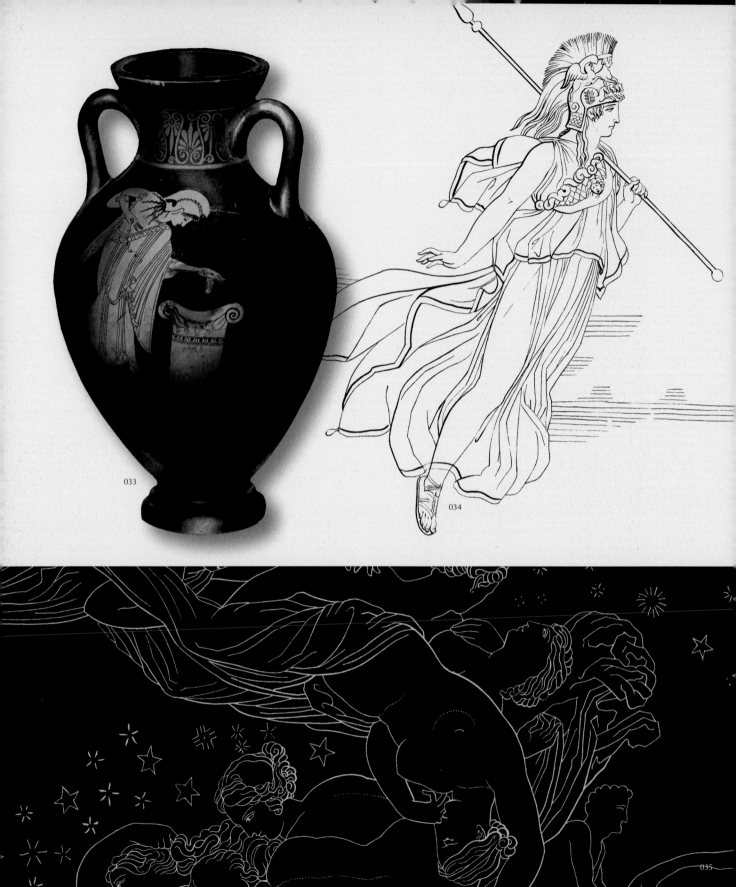

033

034

035

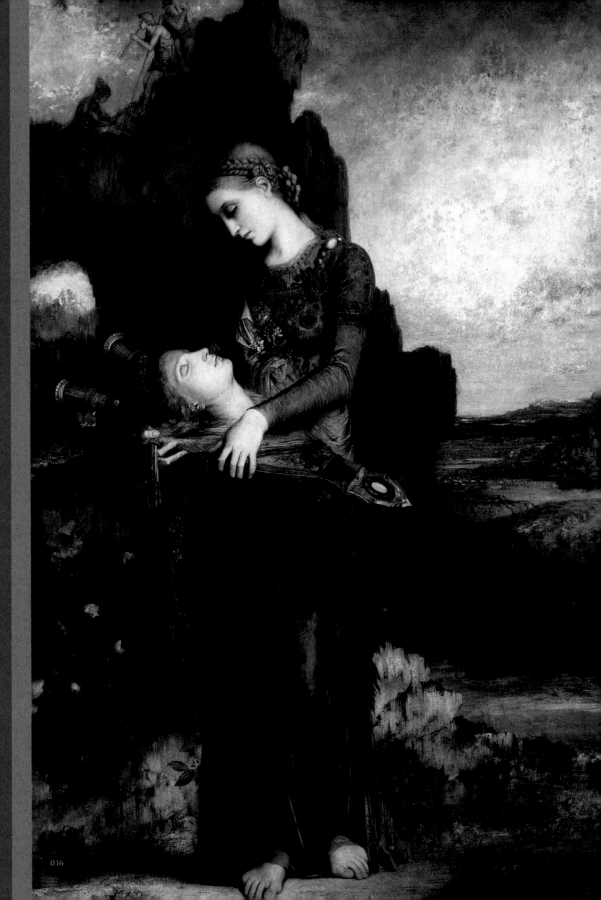

037

038

040

041

043

046

048

049

050

051

053

054 background

060

061

062

064

066

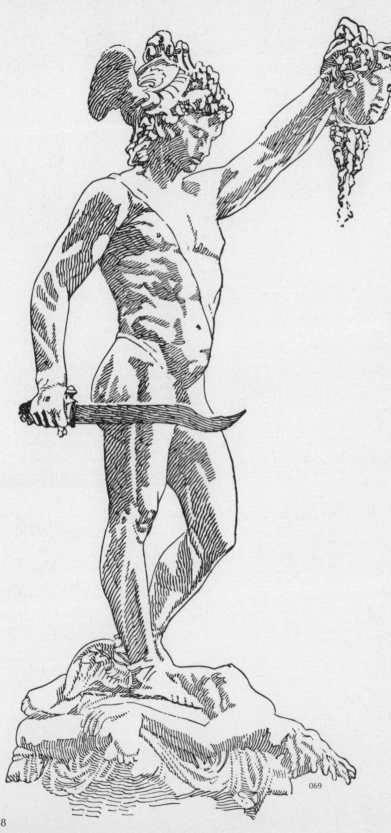

069

070

071

073

074

075

077

078

079

080

081

082

083

084

085

088

071

089

090

091

092

093

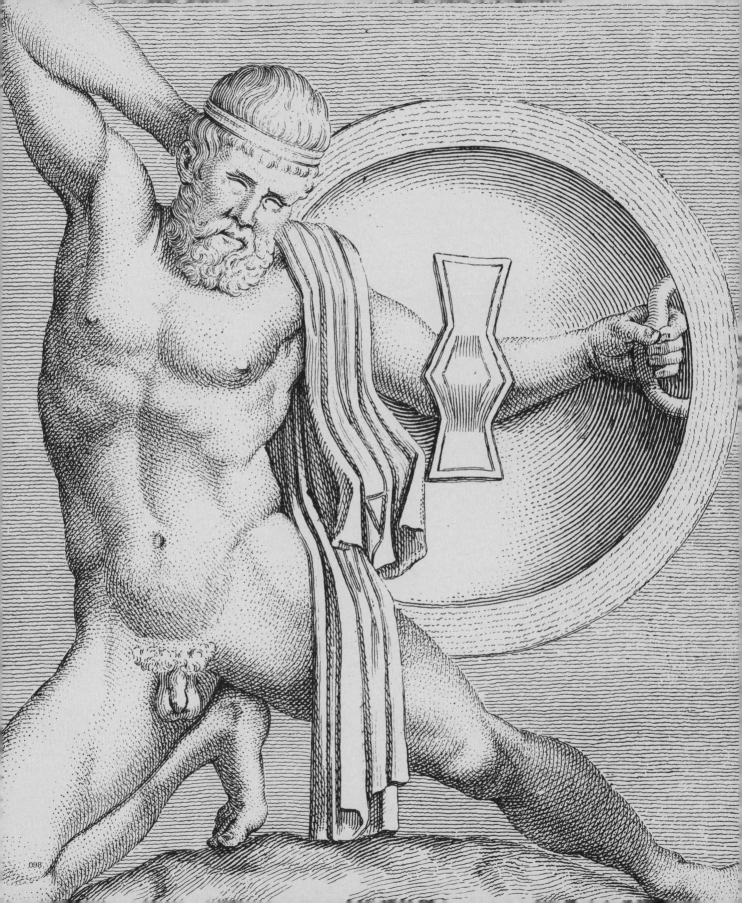

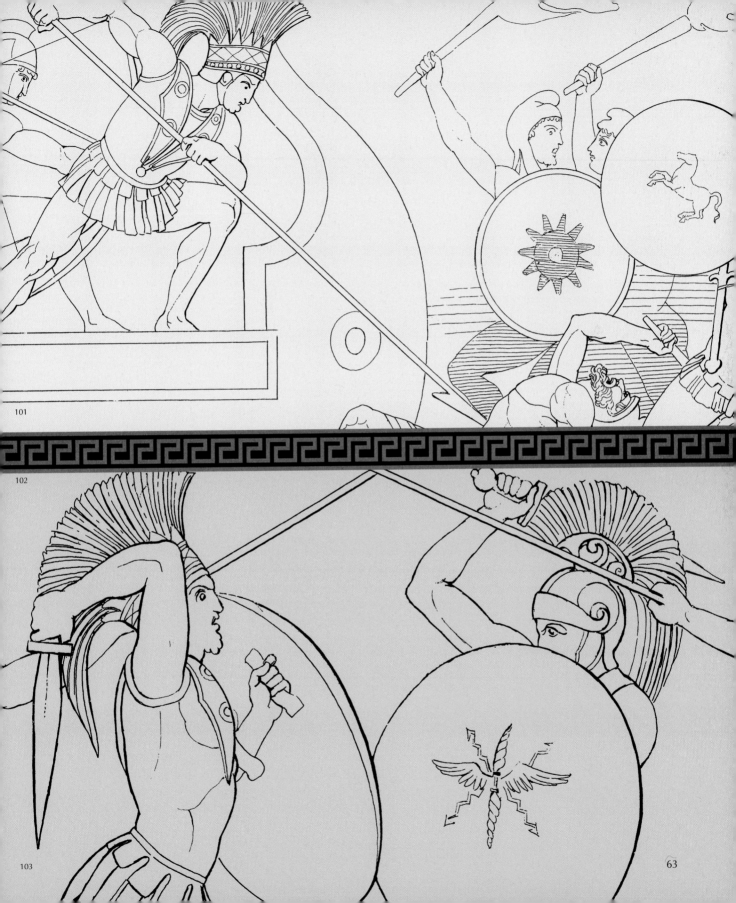

101

102

103

106

107

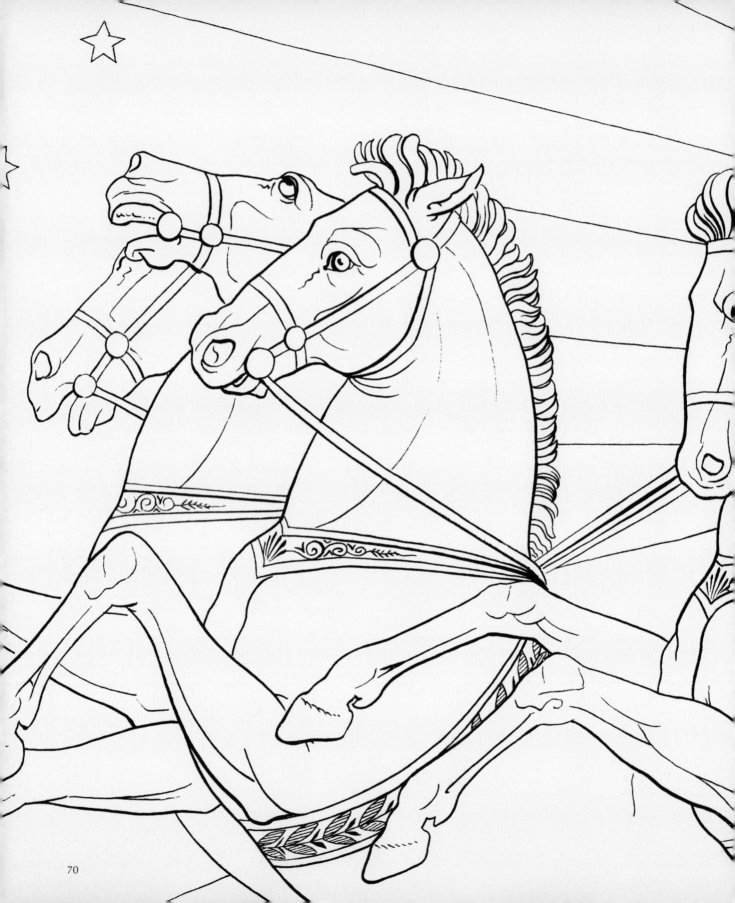

116

117

118

122

124

127

128

129

130

131

132

134 background

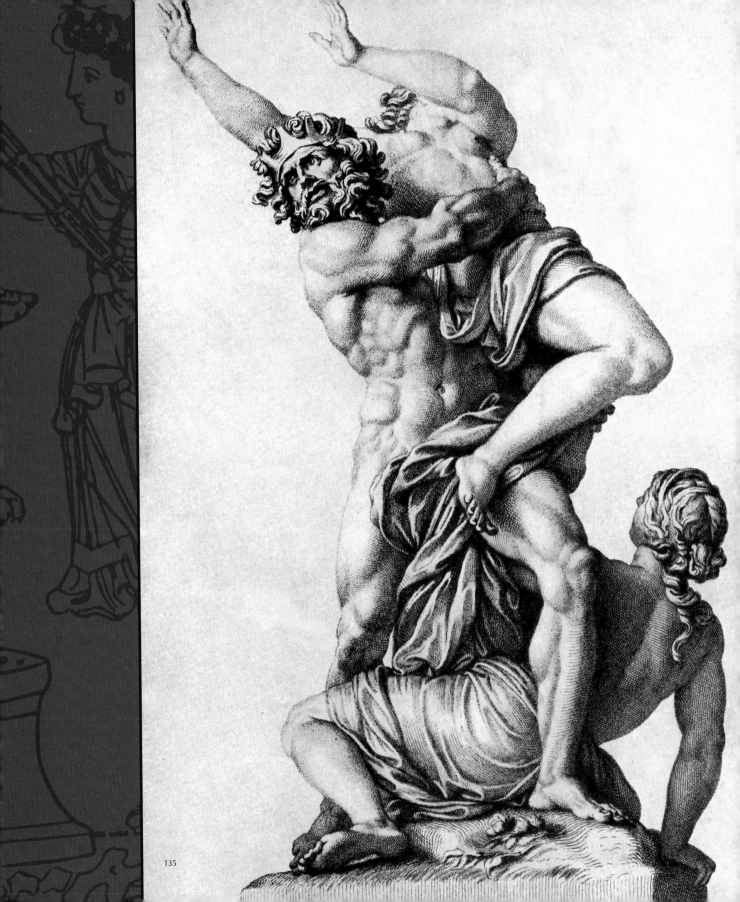

137

138

139

141

142

143

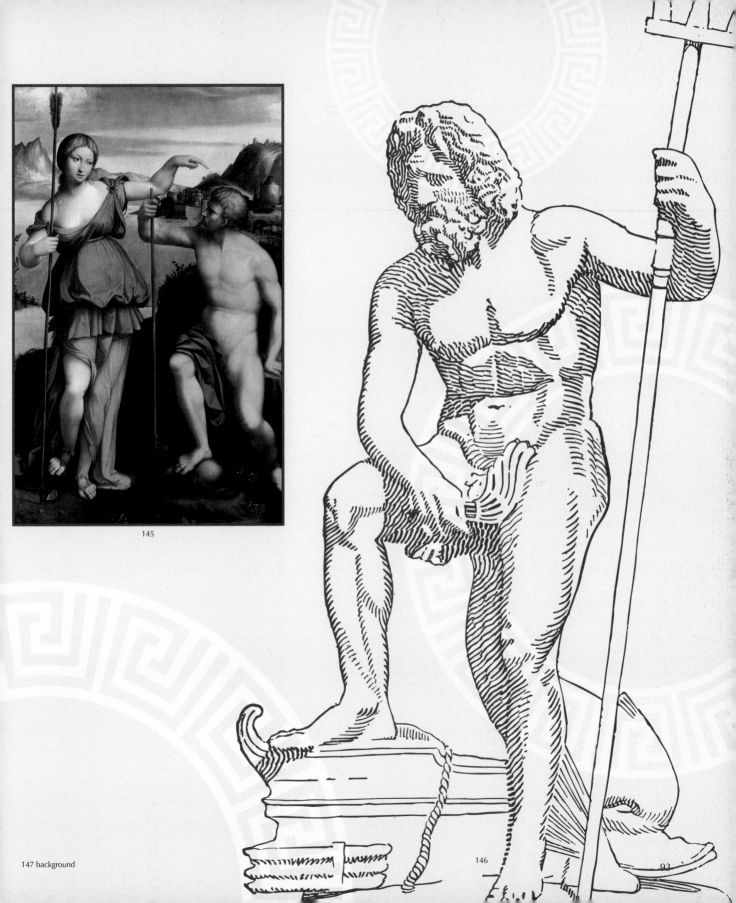

145

147 background

146

148

150

151

152

154

155

159

162

163

165

166

168

172

173

174

177

178 background

179

181

182

183

184

190

195

196 background

197

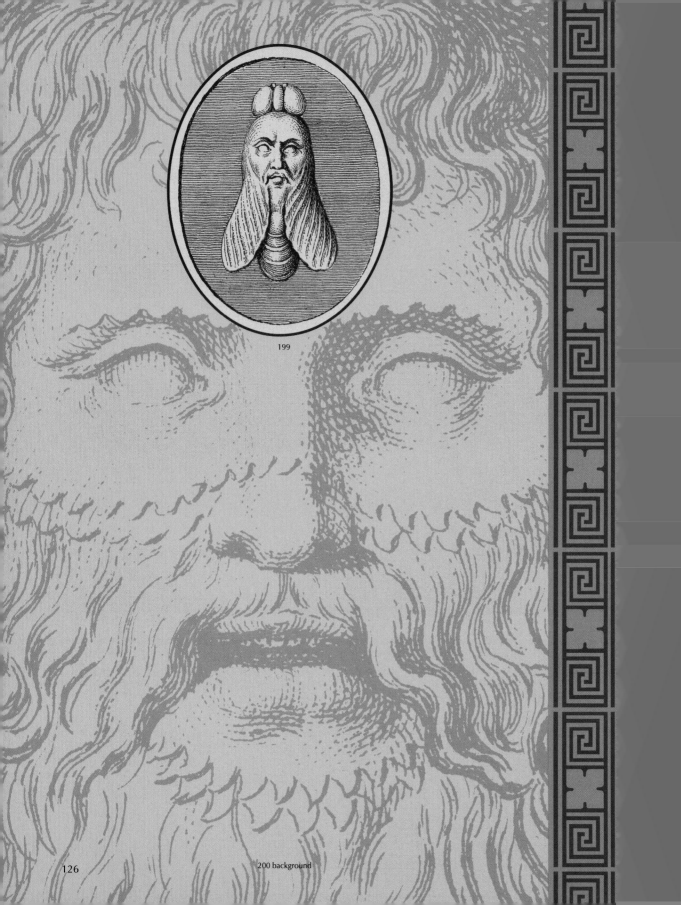

199

200 background

List of Images

List of Vector Images